NATIONAL
GEOGRAPHIC

First, Second, Third

Jan Pritchett

Which skier is **first**?

Which cab is **second**?

Which horse is third?

Which bicycle is fourth?

Which car is **fifth**?

Which camel is **sixth**?

first

second

third

fourth

fifth

sixth